For Wally

First published 1987 by Walker Books Ltd
87 Vauxhall Walk, London SE11 5HJ

This edition published 1992

© 1987 Martin Handford

Printed and bound in Italy by
L.E.G.O., Vicenza

British Library Cataloguing in Publication Data
A catalogue record for this book is available
from the British Library.

ISBN 0-7445-2538-1

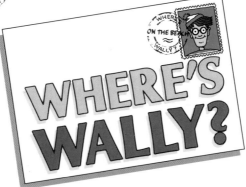

WHERE'S WALLY?

MARTIN HANDFORD

WALKER BOOKS
LONDON

HI FRIENDS!

MY NAME IS WALLY.

I'M JUST SETTING OFF ON A WORLD-WIDE HIKE. YOU CAN COME TOO. ALL YOU HAVE TO DO IS FIND ME, WHEREVER I GO.

I'VE GOT ALL I NEED - WALKING STICK, KETTLE, MALLET, CUP, RUCKSACK, SLEEPING BAG, BINOCULARS, CAMERA, SNORKEL, BELT, BAG AND SHOVEL.

BY THE WAY, I'M NOT TRAVELLING ON MY OWN. THAT'S MY DOG WOOF AND WENDA BEHIND ME, AND TEN WALLY-WATCHERS. WHEREVER I GO, WOOF AND WENDA ARE THERE SOMEWHERE – THOUGH ALL YOU CAN EVER SEE OF WOOF IS HIS TAIL. WATCH OUT FOR THE WALLY-WATCHERS TOO – EACH APPEARS ONCE ON MY TRAVELS.

FIND ALL OF US, IF YOU CAN.

Wally

GREETINGS,
WALLY FOLLOWERS!
WOW, THE BEACH WAS
GREAT TODAY! I SAW
THIS GIRL STICK AN
ICE CREAM IN HER
BROTHER'S FACE, AND
THERE WAS A SAND
CASTLE WITH A REAL
KNIGHT IN ARMOUR
INSIDE! FANTASTIC!

Wally

TO:
WALLY FOLLOWERS,
HERE, THERE,
EVERYWHERE.

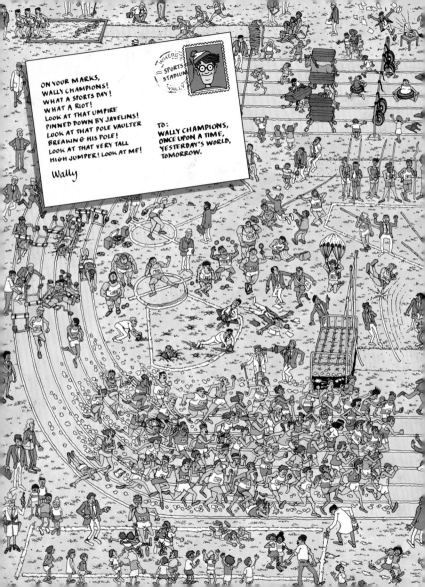

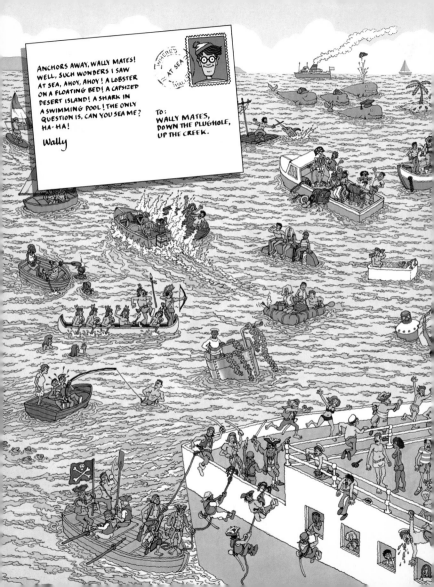

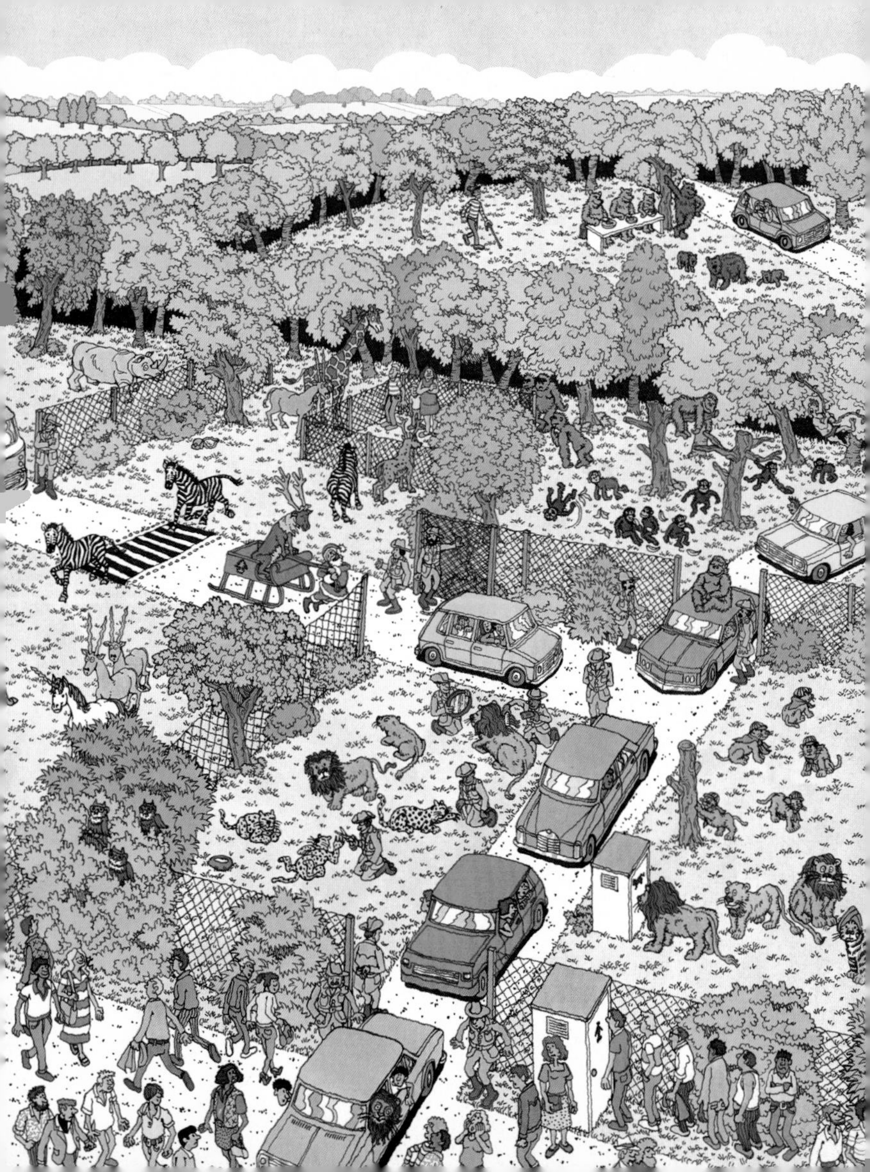

WOTCHA, WALLY WATCHERS!
SAW SOME TRULY TERRIFIC
SIGHTS TODAY - SOMEONE
BURNING TROUSERS WITH
AN IRON; A LONG THIN MAN
WITH A LONG THIN TIE;
A GLOVE ATTACKING A MAN.
PHEW! INCREDIBLE!

Wally

TO:
WALLY WATCHERS,
OVER THE MOON,
THE WILD WEST,
NOW.

ROLL UP, WALLY FUN LOVERS!
WOW, I'VE LOST ALL MY THINGS,
ONE IN EVERY PLACE. NOW YOU
HAVE TO GO BACK AND FIND
THEM. AND WENDA LOST HER
UMBRELLA SOMEWHERE – CAN
ANYBODY FIND IT? WORST OF ALL,
THE BOBBLE'S MISSING FROM ONE
WALLY-WATCHER'S HAT – WHICH
HAT, AND WHERE IS THE BOBBLE?

TO:
WALLY FUN LOVERS,
BACK TO THE BEGINNING,
START AGAIN, TERRIFIC.

Wally

THE GREAT WHERE'S WALLY? CHECK LIST
Hundreds more things for Wally watchers to watch out for!

IN TOWN
- A dog on a roof
- A man on a fountain
- A man about to trip over a dog's lead
- A car crash
- A keen barber
- People in a street, watching TV
- A puncture caused by a Roman arrow
- A tearful tune
- A boy attacked by a plant
- A waiter who isn't concentrating
- A robber who's been clobbered
- A face on a wall
- A man coming out of a man-hole
- A man feeding pigeons
- A bicycle crash

SKI SLOPES
- A man reading on a roof
- A flying skier
- A runaway skier
- A backward skier
- A portrait in snow
- An illegal fisherman
- A snowball in the neck
- Two unconscious skiers
- Two skiers hitting trees
- An Alpine horn
- A snow skier
- A flag collector
- Two very scruffy skiers
- A skier up a tree
- A water skier on snow
- A Yeti
- A skiing reindeer
- A roof jumper
- A heap of skaters

THE RAILWAY STATION
- A boy falling from a train
- A break-down on tracks
- Naughty children on a train roof
- People being knocked over by a door
- A man about to step on a ball
- Three different trains at the same time
- A wheelbarrow pram
- A face on a train
- Five people reading one newspaper
- A struggling bag carrier
- A show-off with suitcases
- A man losing everything from his cases
- A smoking train
- A squeeze on a bench
- A dog tearing a man's trousers
- Fare dodgers
- A hand caught between doors
- A cattle stampede
- A man breaking a weighing machine

ON THE BEACH
- A dog biting a boy's bottom
- A man who is overdressed
- A muscular medallion man
- A popular girl
- A water skier on water
- A stripy photo
- A punctured lilo
- A donkey who likes ice-cream
- A man being squashed
- A punctured beach ball
- A human pyramid
- A human stepping-stone
- Two odd friends
- A cowboy
- A human donkey
- Age and beauty
- A boy who follows in his father's footsteps
- Two men with vests, one without
- A boy being tortured by a spider
- A show-off with sandcastles
- A gang of hat robbers
- An Arab making pyramids
- Three protruding tongues
- Two oddly fitting hats
- An odd couple
- Five sprinters
- A towel with a hole in it
- A punctured hovercraft
- A boy who's not allowed any ice-cream

CAMP SITE
- A bull in a hedge
- Bull horns
- A shark in a canal
- A bull seeing red
- A careless kick
- Tea in a lap
- A low bridge
- People knocked over by a mallet
- A man surprised undressing
- A bicycle tyre about to be punctured
- Camper's camels
- A scarecrow that doesn't work
- A wigwam
- Large biceps
- A collapsed tent
- A smoking barbecue
- A fisherman catching old boots
- A winning penny-farthing
- Boy scouts making fire
- A roller hiker
- A man blowing up a boat
- A camper's butler
- Runners on the road
- A bull chasing children
- Scruffy campers
- Thirsty walkers

SPORTS STADIUM
- Three pairs of feet, sticking out of sand
- A cowboy starting races
- Hopeless hurdlers
- Ten children with fifteen legs
- A record thrower
- A shot-put juggler
- An ear trumpet
- A vaulting horse
- A runner with two wheels
- A parachuting vaulter
- A Scotsman with a caber
- An elephant pulling a rope
- People being knocked over by a hammer
- A gardener
- Three frogmen
- A nude runner
- A bed
- A bandaged boy
- A runner with four legs
- A sunken jumper
- A man with an odd pair of legs
- A man chasing a dog, chasing a cat
- A boy squirting water